DIGITAL AND INFORMATION LITERACY ™

MOBILE PLATFORMS: GETTING INFORMATION ON THE GO

COLIN WILKINSON

rosen publishing's
rosen
central®

New York

Dedicated to my dad, who taught me the allure of technology

Published in 2011 by The Rosen Publishing Group, Inc.
29 East 21st Street, New York, NY 10010

Library of Congress Cataloging-in-Publication Data

Wilkinson, Colin, 1977–
Mobile platforms: getting information on the go / Colin Wilkinson.—1st ed.
  p. cm.—(Digital and information literacy)
Includes bibliographical references and index.
ISBN 978-1-4488-1320-9 (library binding)
ISBN 978-1-4488-2291-1 (pbk.)
ISBN 978-1-4488-2297-3 (6-pack)
1. Mobile computing—Juvenile literature. 2. Wireless communication systems—Juvenile literature. I. Title.
QA76.59.W543 2011
004.165—dc22

2010023682

Manufactured in the United States of America

CPSIA Compliance Information: Batch #W11YA: For further information, contact Rosen Publishing, New York, New York, at 1-800-237-9932.

CONTENTS

INTRODUCTION

Mobile communication devices have come a long way since the original Motorolas of the mid-1980s. These early cell phones were larger than most house phones and boasted a battery life of thirty minutes. Within the past three years alone, we've seen the introduction of Apple's iPhone and iPad, Amazon's Kindle, and the increasingly popular netbook platform. And on the horizon are even more cutting-edge devices and mobile communication technology, including the HP Slate, Windows Phone 7, and the introduction of a new 4G network. These rapidly changing mobile devices are becoming more and more a part of everyday life, turning what was once a luxury for the well-to-do, then a convenience for many, into what is now a near necessity for all. For this reason, it's important to understand not only the use of these devices, but also how to get the most out of them.

This book will cover the capabilities shared by these devices, each one's particular strengths, and some of the differences among them. How mobile devices can help their users communicate in various ways; find information; perform schoolwork; and seek out hobbies, games, and entertainment will also be highlighted. New techniques that have been developed for mobile information gathering via digital photos, text, and audio will be discussed. How to organize, retrieve, and relay this information to others using the very same mobile device that gathered the information will also be described.

Much has changed in the world of mobile communications in the past twenty years, as evidenced here between the Motorola MicroTAC *(left)* and Apple's latest iPhone 4.

Today's smartphones and mobile devices, including the iPhone, BlackBerry Storm, and Android, are powerhouses of productivity and entertainment. Using mobile communication devices properly and effectively for gathering online information is an increasingly valuable and essential skill for success in school, work, and daily life.

Yet using a smartphone or other mobile device also introduces the need for new guidelines relating to digital privacy, security, and etiquette. Knowing when to silence or power off the device is just as important as knowing when and how to use it. And knowing how to communicate with others respectfully—whether face-to-face or digitally—and use and share information responsibly and ethically are vital to the continued security and civility of both the digital and "real" worlds that we all now inhabit.

Chapter 1

The Evolution of Mobile Technology

ast improvements in computer processors, electronics, and networking technology have been made in recent years. These allow a single mobile device to do the job of what not long ago would have required an arsenal of cell phones, personal digital assistants (PDAs), and laptops in one's backpack, shoulder bag, or briefcase. Today, a single, comprehensive, super-powerful, and comparatively tiny Wi-Fi–enabled device easily fits in the palm of one's hand.

A Brief History of the Cell Phone

The first cell phone call was made in 1973 by Motorola manager Dr. Martin Cooper. He is credited as the inventor of the original cell phone, and for his first call he dialed his longtime rivals at Bell Labs. It would be another ten years, however, before cell phones were first made available for sale to the public. The first ones went on sale in Chicago, Illinois, in 1983.

At the time, it was possible for only twenty-three phone calls to be conducted simultaneously within the same calling area, or "cell," which was an

Dr. Martin Cooper shows off a prototype of the first working cell phone, the Motorola DynaTAC. Nearly forty years since the first cell phone call was made, unexpected improvements and exciting new features are still being introduced.

area of 10 square miles (26 square kilometers). The early phones weighed almost 2 pounds (0.91 kilograms) and were 10 inches (25 centimeters) in length. Despite its short battery life, high cost, and bulky design, waiting lists for the device skyrocketed as consumers became excited by the idea of always being reachable by phone. Within a year and a half, the number of cell phone users within the United States reached approximately three hundred thousand.

Originally, cell phones used an analog network that operated in a similar fashion as a CB radio or walkie-talkie. Each cell, then and now, is controlled by a single tower, provides coverage to the surrounding 10 square miles (26 sq. km) or so, and has access to a limited number of frequencies. Unlike traditional walkie-talkies, which are said to be half-duplex—allowing only one user to speak at a time over a single frequency—cell phone communication requires two frequencies. The full-duplex communication found within cell phones dedicates a frequency for each direction of communication. This allows users to speak simultaneously without one user cutting off the voice of the person to whom he or she is speaking. The first generation of nationwide analog cell phone networks, also referred to as 1G, increased capacity to 395 simultaneous conversations within each cell. An additional forty or so frequencies were set aside for non-voice data transfer, such as the signals and information sent by pagers.

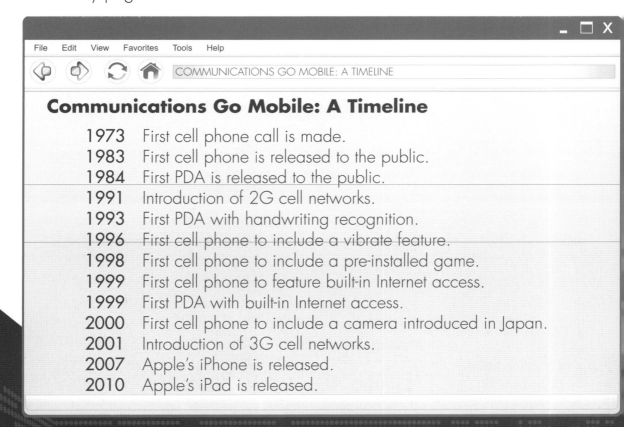

File   Edit   View   Favorites   Tools   Help

COMMUNICATIONS GO MOBILE: A TIMELINE

Communications Go Mobile: A Timeline

1973	First cell phone call is made.
1983	First cell phone is released to the public.
1984	First PDA is released to the public.
1991	Introduction of 2G cell networks.
1993	First PDA with handwriting recognition.
1996	First cell phone to include a vibrate feature.
1998	First cell phone to include a pre-installed game.
1999	First cell phone to feature built-in Internet access.
1999	First PDA with built-in Internet access.
2000	First cell phone to include a camera introduced in Japan.
2001	Introduction of 3G cell networks.
2007	Apple's iPhone is released.
2010	Apple's iPad is released.

Each cell's tower is responsible for handling communications between the individual phone and the broader nationwide and worldwide network of cell phones and landlines. Using a series of identification numbers tied to each phone, cell phone networks can locate a phone by its phone number. It can then determine its carrier company to calculate "roaming" time for calls made outside of the network. The network can also use these identification numbers to smoothly handle the passing along of a call from one cell to another as the mobile phone and its user move between the cells.

The Second Generation

Improvements in the processing power of cell phones brought about the introduction of digital cell phone networks, referred to as 2G, in the early

Palm's two new offerings, the Palm Pre Plus *(left)* and the Palm Pixi Plus, feature the Palm webOS. Both devices introduced in 2010 build on existing models with improved functionality.

1990s. The ability to convert voice to digital signals, and then compress them into a very small amount of data, allowed for up to ten times as many calls to be made within a single cell than was possible within a 1G network. With the advent of digital cell networks came new advantages, such as SMS text messaging and mobile Internet and e-mail access. The new 2G networks also allowed an increased focus on mobile computing known as personal communications services (PCS). In fact, GSM, a popular type of 2G network, still remains an international standard in many areas of the world outside of the Americas.

At this time, cell phone devices were still fairly clunky compared to today's devices. Full-color displays and QWERTY keyboards remained non-existent until the early-2000s. Mobile devices were beginning to outgrow the limitations of the 2G networks as PDAs began merging with cell phones. In the early and mid-2000s, advances in cell phone technology once again spurred faster and more reliable networks. At nearly three times the speed of prior digital networks, 3G networks began to allow users broadband access to the Internet. This development enabled the introduction of smartphones.

State of the Art

For the past decade, smartphones have blurred the lines between cell phones and PDAs. They have provided instant communication and the utility of a desktop organizer in a pocket-sized device. The current generation of devices features integrated e-mail, Web browsing, contact and calendar management, calling, and texting. In addition, a wide array of downloadable applications are available for use with the new devices. These range from games, maps, and global positioning systems (GPS) to productivity enhancements and social networking. At the forefront of this new generation of devices are the BlackBerry, the iPhone, and the Android.

Increasingly, mobile devices are shifting everyday tasks to a digital environment. For example, wireless reading devices are becoming more and more popular. Since the introduction of Amazon's Kindle, which provides near-instant access to a collection of downloadable books, newspapers, and magazines, other companies have followed suit with products such as Barnes & Noble's Nook and Sony's Digital Reader.

These so-called eReaders all feature sharp text display, adjustable font sizes, and a battery life long enough to allow the reading of several books on a single charge. Light, compact electronic reading devices have an edge over heavier printed books for someone on the go who plans to read several books and other kinds of printed publications. With a Wi-Fi connection, the browsing, purchasing, and downloading of books, newspapers, and magazines is quick and easy.

Laptop computers, already prized for their portability, have seen a trend toward even greater mobility. New types of laptops, such as ultra-portable computers or netbooks, seek to provide all of the functionality of a desktop computer in a tiny, lightweight package. These computers are made so small and light by minimizing the screen and keyboard dimensions. Despite their small size, they retain utility by removing large and energy-intensive components like a CD-ROM or DVD drive. They instead rely on Internet access for streaming music and video. By using smaller and less powerful processors and solid state storage mediums, these ultra-portable laptops and netbooks require fewer cooling components. This frees up power and space for other functions and reduces overall size.

The march of progress in mobile communications and computing seems unstoppable. New devices are always being developed and introduced to meet the evolving demands of the consumer market and to take advantage of the latest technological advances. These advances and the devices that harness them expand the range of possibilities for how, where, and even why we communicate with one another. For example, new touch devices, such as Apple's iPad, the HP Slate, and the ASUS EeeKeyboard, bridge the gap between a smartphone and laptop with a new balance of mobility and power. While these devices lean more toward the features of a laptop and don't include the ability to make and receive calls, they do open up new possibilities for mobile communicators.

New devices, such as Apple's iPad, bridge the gap between mobile computing and mobile communications. Smaller and faster chipsets, touch screens combining keyboards and displays, and stronger wireless capabilities continue to broaden the potential of today's devices.

Upcoming smartphones, such as the Windows Phone 7, promise to bring more familiar user experience and computing power to the handheld market. And looming on the horizon is the fourth generation of cellular wireless standards—4G networks—featuring mobile ultra-broadband access and multicarrier transmission.

MYTHS & FACTS

MYTH Cell phones emit radiation that may cause cancer.

FACT Electromagnetic radiation emitted from a cell phone is not strong enough to cause cancer. In fact, all electronic devices emit a miniscule amount of harmless radiation.

MYTH Cell phones may cause hospital equipment to malfunction.

FACT To date, there has been no evidence of this, even after extensive studies. However, it's still important to follow any posted guidelines prohibiting cell phone use.

MYTH Cell phones may cause interference with an airplane's electronics.

FACT According to extensive research conducted by both the Federal Aviation Administration (FAA) and the National Aeronautics and Space Administration (NASA), there is little-to-no possibility that a cell phone signal could disrupt aircraft electronics, although they maintain the "better safe than sorry" stance.

Chapter 2

A User's Guide to Mobile Devices

While the technology driving smartphones is constantly evolving, the actual controls of any new device must remain intuitive enough that a broad range of users will feel comfortable enough to buy it. At the same time, each individual user has particular needs that he or she wants a mobile device to meet.

One of these needs is the ability to use a mobile device for schoolwork and research. Having a user-friendly mobile device as an information-gathering tool means students can do their homework, conduct group projects, research their papers, and get their questions answered anywhere they happen to be, at any time. What follows is an overview of how to use some of the exciting new methods of group communication and information gathering made possible by mobile communication devices for schoolwork.

Organizing Contacts

Today's mobile communication devices make it easy to keep the contact information of friends, family, acquaintances, and project partners

NEW MESSAGE

TO: STAFF
FROM: CEO
All employee meeting in
15 minutes in large
conference room.

Mobile devices allow for instant communication via voice or text between coworkers, classmates, friends, and family members.

organized, thanks to their built-in contacts applications. The contacts app can be used not just to store names and numbers, but also mailing addresses, e-mail addresses, instant messaging accounts, and even pictures. Best of all, contacts apps have built-in notes fields, allowing for additional information to be added as needed.

Adding a new contact is easy. The BlackBerry Storm, iPhone, and Android all include a prominent plus sign button on the touch screen for adding new contacts. Simply hit the button and follow the prompts for adding contact information. Additionally, individual contacts may be organized into various groups. For example, the contact information for all the members of a specific school project can be placed in one group. This allows the user to access the complete roster of project members with one click. Similarly, the contact information of frequently visited libraries and other research centers can be placed in one group for quick reference.

To manage groups on the BlackBerry Storm, begin by pressing the Menu key and then touching the New Group button to create a group. Using the Menu key again, contacts may be added to the current group. With the iPhone, groups can be accessed by hitting the Groups button in the top left of the screen. Yet managing groups cannot be done directly on the device. Creating and editing groups of contacts must be done within Apple's Address Book application using a laptop or desktop computer and then synced to the device. Similarly, group management on the Android must be done within the Gmail interface, either on a computer or through the device's browser.

Making Conference Calls and Multitasking

Collecting useful information during phone calls made on the go is not always easy. Nor is speaking to two or more people who are all speaking from different locations. Yet today's smartphones make remote group discussions and conference calls easier than ever. They also provide many tools designed to make note- and recordkeeping during these calls an efficient and pain-free process.

Many of today's devices include speakerphone capabilities, three-way calling, and the ability to access other applications and information on the device while making a call.

One such feature is the ability to run a conference call with three or sometimes more members directly from the device. Such a call can be essential to information sharing within a group that may not always be able to meet in person, such as when working on a team project. To create a conference call, start by calling the first participant. To add a second participant from a BlackBerry Storm, touch the Add Participant button (or Add Call on the iPhone and Android), dial in the number of the second person, and hit the Send key. To create and join the conference, hit the Menu key and touch the Join Conference button (or Merge Calls on the iPhone and Android).

One of the more exciting smartphone utilities is the ability to use the device for other purposes even while still using it to hold a conversation. This kind of multitasking can be achieved by using the speakerphone option, toggled with the on-screen Speaker button (or by pressing the Menu key and then the Speaker button on an Android device). With the speakerphone enabled, the phone can be operated away from the user's face. It can instead be held in front of the user or placed down on a table. This allows the user to keep speaking while also using the device's touch screen to search for information, open files, send e-mails or texts, surf the Web, or take notes on what is being said.

Text Communications

Today's smartphones provide a number of ways to communicate instantly via text. One of the most popular is by using SMS text messages. The ability to send and receive text messages is handled by software already installed on the device. Begin by activating the messaging application on the device and touch the Compose button to create a new message. On the iPhone, this appears as an icon on the top right, while on the Android it appears at the top of the screen with a "New Message" label. To choose the recipient(s), enter his or her cell phone number or choose the person from the contacts list. Once the message has been typed, hit Send to deliver it. Historically, SMS messages were limited to 160 characters. However, today's devices allow for longer messages by splitting them up before delivery. The separated messages are then joined together again in the proper order when received.

When communication needs require more text—and more complex text—than can easily fit within a text message, e-mail is the more suitable option. Sending an e-mail works similarly to sending a text message. But the e-mail is delivered to an e-mail address over the Internet, rather than to a phone number. The process is the same as it is when sending an e-mail from a computer. In order to send and receive e-mail, the mobile device must first have one or more e-mail accounts set up. This is done through the Settings on the iPhone and the Setup application on the Storm. The Android will prompt the user for this information the first time its e-mail application is run. Incoming text and e-mail messages display as alerts on the mobile devices and can be read within their messaging applications.

Finding Resources Online

One of the best uses of modern smartphones is as an ultra-mobile Internet access point with broadband, for rapid information and research retrieval. The browsing applications found on today's smartphones replicate nearly all the abilities of their computer counterparts. This

Texts and e-mail can be great ways to communicate, but finding the right time to catch up on messages is an important skill to learn as part of today's mobile lifestyle.

includes bookmarking, browsing history, and integrated Web searching. Additionally, sharing Web pages and other information with people entered into the device's contacts listings is made simple with direct access to e-mail or text URLs.

File   Edit   View   Favorites   Tools   Help

TIPS AND TRICKS

Tips and Tricks

- Typing on a full QWERTY keyboard is often much faster than using a numeric pad. Also, rotating your device to landscape mode will often provide a larger keyboard for input.
- Don't overlook your device settings—many powerful options are hidden within them.
- When adding contacts, use custom fields to track additional information. You can then search for contacts that include that particular information.
- Use your phone's search ability to quickly find contacts, messages, Web page bookmarks, and media stored to your device.
- Add notes to existing calendar events to track progress and record the outcomes of your appointments.

To access a Web site, simply enter the browser application from the device's applications list. Then enter a URL into the location bar or a search phrase into the search field. Many Web sites now include dedicated alternate layouts. These are designed to take advantage of a smartphone's small screen and touch interface and will load automatically upon detecting the mobile device.

Documenting to Digital

When doing research in a library, it can be beneficial to digitally record notes, memos, and research findings using a smartphone. Using the phone's camera or a voice recording application can be a great way to quickly document ideas and take notes to be followed up on later. For example,

Today's devices allow users to do more than communicate via text or voice. Using photos or even video to capture a moment can be a fun and unique way to share an experience with friends.

you could photograph a page of text from a book, map, or other graphic. Or you could quietly record some ideas for other books to investigate later or facts to check.

Taking pictures is a snap on today's devices. The camera application does most of the work for you. Access the device's camera application by tapping its icon. Use the screen to frame the shot and be sure to hold the device still. The rest is just point and shoot.

A picture may be worth a thousand words, but sometimes it doesn't quite do the job. The Voice Memos feature of the iPhone, or the Voice Notes

Recorder on the BlackBerry Storm, can be used for hands-free notetaking. Voice notes may be stored and played back directly on the device. They can even be shared with teammates or group project members. Although the Android does not include a built-in voice memo application, a free application may be downloaded to the Android from the Market.

Managing Time

Today's smartphones include detailed calendars. These calendars often have the ability to sync up with online calendar services or existing calendars on a computer. This allows the user to have all the same scheduling information on

Using sync functionality, users can make sure that changes to calendars, notes, and other data are made across devices.

all the calendars he or she refers to. Each mobile device's calendar application allows viewing and managing of multiple calendars. For instance, a calendar can be created for home and personal activities, while another can be used for school and work. It is even possible to import the calendars of friends, family members, teammates, and group project members.

Adding events and appointments to a calendar is a straightforward, step-by-step process. It is achieved by launching the Calendar application and pressing the New Event button on the device's screen (or by pressing the Menu key on the BlackBerry Storm). Existing events may be viewed and organized by day, week, and month. Stay on top of upcoming events by setting reminders within the calendar. The phone's ringtone will alert the user to the upcoming event.

For more fine-grained time management, the clock application found on the iPhone and BlackBerry Storm provides the ability to set daily alarms. It also allows for a stopwatch or countdown timer to help track time spent on specific project tasks. While the Android's built-in alarm clock application allows only for alarms to be set, several free applications are available within the Market that provide stopwatch and timer functionality.

Chapter 3

The Wide World of Mobile Apps

Never has expanding the utility of a mobile communication device been so easy as it is today. Downloadable applications for smartphones have become commonplace. They allow customization through a massive catalog of productivity software, games, and utilities. Accessing and using the iPhone and iPad App Store (or Market for the Android and App World for the BlackBerry Storm) have been made very straightforward. They all offer user-friendly features such as quick searches, top downloads, and categorized lists of applications. To start, simply touch the store icon on the device and begin browsing the available apps. To download and install an app, simply touch the Download or Buy button.

What follows are descriptions of some of the more popular and useful applications available for today's mobile devices.

Productivity

One of the most common tasks when working at a computer is document editing. So it is no wonder that this has become a popular focus of mobile

Before downloading an app, it is important to do some research. Check user ratings and reviews, product descriptions, and look for a demo first. Make sure the software will do the job needed before purchasing or downloading it.

apps. Numerous apps allow text and spreadsheet documents to be read and even edited on the go via mobile devices. These include Documents 2 Free for iPhone and Documents to Go for BlackBerry Storm.

Invaluable tools when working within documents include translation utilities, dictionaries, and spell-checkers, all of which have made an appearance on mobile platforms. Apps like Android Translator allow translation of text to and from multiple languages. Advanced apps, such as Navita Translator, will go as far as to speak translated phrases. Popular free services, such as Dictionary.com, have begun offering apps for smartphones. These are a great reference resource for definitions, synonyms, and even spelling correction.

An important aspect of working as a team is idea sharing. Several new collaborative note-taking applications have been developed. One of the most popular is Evernote. This app is designed to make it easy to record and later recall everything that is said in a lecture, lab, or group meeting.

Geographical apps, including Google Maps and Google Earth, can prove invaluable when planning a trip. As up-to-date as these apps are, they can't always keep up with changes in traffic patterns and new construction.

Evernote allows the creation of text, voice, or photographic notes. These notes can then be uploaded to a computer or shared via e-mail with others.

Another popular method for sharing files and information from mobile devices and computers is via the free online service Dropbox. At its heart, Dropbox is an online file storage system. What makes it unique, however, is the ease with which it allows the user to post and retrieve files from a smartphone. Dropbox allows not only for sharing files with friends and colleagues, but also for sharing information across multiple computers and mobile devices. This makes it easy to work on a single file from home, at the school library, or on a mobile device, depending on which is most convenient at any given time.

For those accustomed to using the popular all-in-one Web service Google, the Google Mobile app provides access to e-mail, calendars, documents, chat, translation tools, maps, and more. Unique mobile features for the suite include search-by-voice, location-aware maps and directions, and integrated voicemail.

Given all of the different types of tasks that can be accomplished on a smartphone, a must-have app for every user should be a well-organized to-do list. Apps such as Tag-ToDo-List and ToDo Lite make this easy by allowing the user to organize tasks into categories, prioritize tasks, and set due dates.

Internet and Social Apps

Online communication has been made increasingly easy with the introduction of mobile versions of popular social networking and instant messaging (IM) apps. In fact, some of the most popular messaging applications even come pre-installed on purchased smartphones. AOL Instant Messenger, for instance, is available across all platforms. Even if a particular IM network doesn't have a dedicated app for a particular device, Meebo is typically there to help fill in the gaps. Meebo is a Web platform for IM on any network or site. By using either Meebo's Web interface or its dedicated app, it is possible to chat across multiple networks from one streamlined interface.

When text-based communication just isn't fast enough, group voice chat may serve the purpose. Skype has become the app of choice in this area, allowing for free conference calling over the Internet. This means that no calling plan minutes are used. Working in a similar way to other popular chat applications, Skype offers a contact list that tracks friends and their online status. With a quick touch of the screen, new text or voice chat rooms can be created for one-on-one or group discussions. Group communication apps such as this can become essential when working remotely with a team.

Smart Purchases

While there is a free app out there for almost any need and interest, advanced features and improved usability sometimes come at an additional development cost. When it seems like only a paid app will do the job, follow these purchasing guidelines:

1. If possible, download a demo or lite version of the app for free in order to try it out before purchasing it.
2. Read the reviews before purchasing. This can often be a great way to find out what makes an app great—or not so great.
3. Review the price of any app before purchasing and verify that whoever is paying for it (if not yourself) can afford the purchase and is willing to make it. These purchases may be charged to the monthly phone bill or directly to a credit card.
4. Test out the app after purchase, and download it to ensure it's working properly. Not all app stores have return policies, and some may have time limits after which a return cannot be made.

To keep up with friends' activities and share your own, social networking sites provide an entirely new form of online communication. Information can now be shared instantaneously among friends at any time, from anywhere, with the use of Internet-enabled smartphones. Both Facebook and Twitter provide apps for today's mobile devices, as well as accessible Web interfaces. These apps add some additional features tailored to the abilities of the particular mobile device, including integrated alerts and improved touch screen control. With additional support for built-in GPS functionality on the device, some apps allow users to track not just their friends' activities, but

Applications like Pandora are blurring the lines between entertainment and social networking. Tim Westergren, founder of Pandora Media, Inc., appears above.

their location as well. All of these innovations allow friends and family members to stay in touch, post personal updates, share news and photos, and arrange meeting places and times.

Creativity

When users get their hands on a pocket-sized, touch-controllable device, it is not long before it becomes an outlet for creative expression—and a means to share that creative output. Some leading painting and drawing apps include Scribble Lite on iPhone, Make a Mess on BlackBerry Storm, and Zebra Paint on Android. They can be a great way to quickly sketch an idea, add illustrative notes to photos, or paint like a pro. In addition to drawing apps, the built-in camera found on today's mobile devices has created a demand for photography and photo-editing apps among amateurs and professionals alike. For example, LEGO Photo for iPhone turns photos into toy mosaics, while PicSay for Android includes tools for color correction and adding word balloons to photos.

Entertainment

Many apps have gained popularity by providing a welcome and entertaining distraction between classes, study sessions, or other periods of work. Some of these apps can even enhance schoolwork and research. Software versions of digital readers, such as Amazon's Kindle and Barnes & Noble's Nook, allow the downloading of fiction and reference books. Many of these are available for free.

Free music-streaming apps, including Last.fm and Pandora Radio, provide recommendations based on music and genre preferences. Even video streaming is available on today's mobile devices using free apps like YouTube. App stores have also started to stock a wealth of quality, free games. Available games range from classics, like chess for Android, to high action titles, such as Flight Path for BlackBerry Storm.

Chapter 4

Etiquette on the Go

There is a new freedom to communicate with others via a mobile device from nearly anywhere, to nearly anywhere, and at any time. With this freedom comes the equal responsibility to understand how these interactions should properly be conducted and when they are and are not appropriate. Improper use of a cell phone can get the user into trouble, result in unwanted charges on the phone bill, or lead to inadvertent hurt feelings. Knowing when to refrain from cell phone usage is an important social skill expected of all users.

Power Down

Following posted regulations remains one of the easiest methods to avoid most problems resulting from inappropriate usage of mobile devices. Taking a call in a movie theater can disrupt everyone else's enjoyment, as can simply reading e-mails and texts, since the screen light is distracting. Using mobile devices on an airplane during the times in the flight when it is

Signs like this one are becoming more common in public places and should be observed for everyone's benefit.

forbidden can even lead to arrest. If it is unclear if usage of a cell phone or other mobile device is allowed at a particular time in a particular place, it's better to ask than to assume.

One of the most basic of mobile device etiquette rules revolves around common sense: if the lights are dimmed or off in a room, the cell phone should be as well. This simple guideline will help avoid unwanted distractions and disruptions for those around you at restaurants, movie theaters, and performances. Similarly, it is important to be aware of the needs of others. When in a dedicated quiet or study area, such as a school library, cell phones should be silenced or powered off. Scheduling a "no cell phone" period of time each day can also be helpful to prevent distractions and provide additional focus for schoolwork and other activities. Later, after the work is done, missed calls, voice mail, e-mail, and text messages can be checked and responded to.

When a call comes in that cannot be ignored, it's important to properly excuse oneself from any conversation or activity. Additionally, it is often wise to find a quiet and private location to talk—not everyone enjoys being forced to overhear the phone conversations of others. When taking a call that is interrupting other activities, keep the call short and avoid dividing one's attention. And it doesn't hurt to let everyone know that the call will just take a minute. Don't hesitate to let the caller know if he or she is interrupting something, but be sure to give that person the attention he or she needs.

In many places, a loud, startling, or otherwise disruptive ringtone can become a huge distraction and source of annoyance for those around you. When possible, switching the device's ringer to a vibrate-only mode can effectively avoid these situations while still alerting the user to an important incoming call. Remember, too, that today's cell phones contain sophisticated microphones and software that can distinguish the voice from ambient background sounds. This means that users no longer have to shout into the phone to be heard by the person on the other end. Maintaining a normal indoor speaking volume is both adequate for being heard on the other end and polite to those around you. There is no need to yell and no need to share a conversation with anyone who happens to be nearby.

Being Aware and Taking Care

Bandwidth comes with a cost, and it's important to be aware of what costs may be accrued through device usage. Depending on a device's plan, there is likely a limited number of minutes with which to make calls each month. And the same goes for messaging and Internet usage. These costs typically increase when roaming off of the network. Additional charges may be applied against the recipient of a call or text message as well. A good practice is to verify friends' cell plans before sending text messages to them and possibly costing them money.

When borrowing someone else's mobile device, special care must be taken to avoid additional charges to that person's account, changing his or her settings, and accidentally accessing private information. Always ask for permission before borrowing someone's device, and be sure to clarify what activities you are permitted to perform on the device. It's also important to set clear ground rules and guidelines when lending a device to another person.

Cite Your Sources

Using a mobile device to gather information and research is no different from using a computer or a library. The same rules regarding the use of

Unfortunately, many cell phone plans come with hidden costs. Always get the OK from the person responsible for paying the bills before taking advantage of a mobile device's features. When uncertain, it's always best to ask first.

copyrighted material, plagiarism, and the citing of sources apply. Text and images found online may be copyrighted and should never be reprinted without citation or permission. To cite sources properly, it's useful to record not only the information that is found, but also the location where it was found. For instance, bookmarking Web pages is important when using content from them. Credit should always be given when citing sources, and luckily the powerful features found within smartphones help streamline this process.

Think Before You Text, and Stay Safe

Instant access to social networks and online community services can make it easy to post ideas and comments instantly. However, this comes with several cautions. Just like taking a deep, calming breath to collect and organize thoughts before speaking, it is important to review e-mails and texts before sending or posting them.

Unfortunately, the negative aspects of online communication can sometimes extend to mobile communications as well. Cyberbullying can occur via text messages, e-mails, and harassing phone calls—all sent from mobile devices. Because mobile devices often contain so much personal identifying information, cell phone theft can often result in identity theft. Online dating conducted via a mobile device can, in some circumstances, lead to abuse, deception, harassment, and stalking. In the case of receiving unwelcome text messages or phone calls, the best advice is not to respond. Keep a log of when the messages are received and, if it is known, whom they are coming from. Share this information with parents or another trusted adult.

Before responding to inappropriate or offensive messages, take a moment to think calmly about what is the proper response and how to best defuse the situation.

Always keep private information secure. Be aware of your surroundings when engaging in a private conversation in public. Only offer sensitive and personal identifying information like a Social Security or credit card number to trusted and reputable companies and organizations. And if giving this information verbally over a cell phone, do so quietly so that no one near you hears. If need be, wait until a more private conversation can be held to avoid inadvertently sharing personal and sensitive information with others standing nearby.

The brave new world of mobile communication devices allows users to text and call friends, set up conference calls with group project members, surf the Internet, access research libraries, compose and edit text, take photos, download audio and video files, and explore the possibilities of thousands of other applications. All of this can be performed anywhere, at any time, with the help of a tiny device that fits in the palm of one's hand or in a jacket pocket. Yet this brave new world also has all the same dangers as those found in the real world—crime, harassment, identity theft, bullying, plagiarism, and antisocial behavior. With the enormous freedom offered by mobile devices comes an equally great responsibility to use this new power responsibly, legally, and respectfully.

TEN GREAT QUESTIONS
TO ASK A DIGITAL LIBRARIAN

1   What apps can help me organize my schoolwork and schedules?

2   How can I organize and quickly find the information I store on my device?

3   What apps allow me to access major library collections?

4   How can I access and view newspapers and magazines on my phone?

5   How can I share my work with fellow project members using my device?

6   How can I best track the time I spend on projects and activities using my device?

7   What apps allow me to migrate "hard copy" information to my device?

8   What broadband network or cell phone services should I be looking for from a service provider?

9   How can I extend my device's battery life?

10   What is the best way to back up my phone's data?

GLOSSARY

3G Third generation of cellular networks; a family of standards for mobile telecommunications. 3G services include wide-area wireless voice telephone, video calls, and wireless data, all in a mobile environment.

carrier Cell phone network provider.

full-duplex Two-way network traffic allowing for simultaneous communication between two or more speakers.

GPS Global positioning system; a satellite-based global navigation system that provides highly accurate information regarding one's location and the local time.

GSM Global system for mobile communications; a form of 2G network. "2G" stands for second-generation wireless telephone technology, which featured services such as digitally encrypted phone conversations and SMS text messaging.

half-duplex Two-way network traffic allowing for communication in only one direction at a time, such as on a walkie-talkie.

MMS Multimedia messaging service; the standard way to send messages that include multimedia content, such as photos, video, audio, text pages, or ringtones.

network Collection of telecommunication hardware enabling wireless communication.

PCS Personal communications service; the radio band used for digital mobile phone service in North America.

PDA Personal digital assistant; also known as palmtop computers, PDAs are mobile devices that manage one's personal information (calendar, address book, contacts, etc.) and can connect to the Internet.

QWERTY Standard English keyboard layout, named for the first five letters that appear on the keyboard's top row of letters.

roaming Mobile service occurring outside of one's original network; often additional charges apply when roaming.

smartphone Mobile phone that includes features similar to those of a PDA or computer.

SMS Short message service; a part of the GSM mobile communication system that allows for the exchange of short text messages between mobile phone devices.

SNS Social network service; Web-based sites that seek to reflect and build social relations and social networks among people. Some of the leading social network sites include Facebook, Twitter, Classmates.com, MySpace, and LinkedIn.

FOR MORE INFORMATION

Computers for Youth
322 Eighth Avenue, Floor 12A
New York, NY 10001
(212) 563-7300
Web site: http://www.cfy.org
Computers for Youth provides inner-city students with home computers and
    provides training, technical support, and online training so that students
    can do better in school.

Educational Computing Organization of Ontario (ECOO)
10 Morrow Avenue, Suite 202
Toronto, ON M6R 2J1
Canada
(416) 489-1713
Web site: http://www.ecoo.org
The ECOO helps teachers and students in coordinating computer learning
    into the educational process.

Family Online Safety Institute
624 Ninth Street NW, Suite 222
Washington, DC 20001
(202) 775-0158
Web site: http://www.fosi.org
The Family Online Safety Institute is an international, nonprofit organization
    that works to develop a safer Internet for children and families. It works
    to influence public policies and educate the public.

Get Net Wise
Internet Education Foundation

1634 I Street NW
Washington, DC 20009
Web site: http://www.getnetwise.org
Get Net Wise is part of the Internet Education Foundation, which works to
    provide a safe online environment for children and families.

International Society for Technology in Education (ITSE)
1710 Rhode Island Avenue NW, Suite 900
Washington, DC 20036
(866) 654-4777
Web site: http://www.iste.org
The ISTE is the trusted source for professional development, knowledge
    generation, advocacy, and leadership for innovation. A nonprofit
    membership organization, ISTE provides leadership and service to
    improve teaching, learning, and school leadership by advancing the
    effective use of technology in PreK–12 and teacher education.

International Technology and Engineering Educators Association (ITEEA)
1914 Association Drive, Suite 201
Reston, VA 20191-1539
(703) 860-2100
Web site: http://www.iteaconnect.org
The ITEEA promotes technology education and literacy.

Internet Education Foundation
1634 I Street NW, Suite 1100
Washington, DC, 20006
(202) 637-0968
Web site: http://neted.org

The Internet Education Foundation is a nonprofit organization dedicated to
    informing the public about Internet education.

Internet Keep Safe Coalition
1401 K Street NW, Suite 600
Washington, DC 20005
(866) 794-7233
Web site: http://www.ikeepsafe.org
The Internet Keep Safe Coalition is an educational resource for children and
    families that educates about Internet safety and ethics associated with
    Internet technologies.

i-Safe, Inc.
5900 Pasteur Court, Suite #100
Carlsbad, CA 92008
(760) 603-7911
Web site: http://www.isafe.org
Founded in 1998, i-SAFE, Inc., is the leader in Internet safety education.
    Available in all fifty states, Washington, D.C., and Department of
    Defense schools located across the world, i-SAFE is a nonprofit foun-
    dation whose mission is to educate and empower youth to make their
    Internet experiences safe and responsible. The goal is to educate
    students on how to avoid dangerous, inappropriate, or unlawful
    online behavior.

Media Awareness Network
1500 Merivale Road, 3rd Floor
Ottawa, ON K2E 6Z5
Canada

(613) 224-7721
Web site: http://www.media-awareness.ca
The Media Awareness Network creates media literacy programs for young
    Canadians. The site contains educational games about the Internet
    and media.

Public Safety Canada
Attn: Public Safety Portal - SafeCanada.ca
269 Laurier Avenue
West Ottawa, ON K1A 0P8
Canada
(800) 755-7047
Web site: http://www.safecanada.ca
SafeCanada is part of the Canadian government's online efforts to make
    Canada a safe place for all its citizens wherever they are—including
    when they visit cyberspace.

Web Sites

Due to the changing nature of Internet links, Rosen Publishing has developed
an online list of Web sites related to the subject of this book. This site is
updated regularly. Please use this link to access the list:

http://www.rosenlinks.com/dil/mopl

FOR FURTHER READING

Bailey, Diane. *Cyber Ethics*. New York, NY: Rosen Publishing Group, 2008.

Firestone, Mary. *Wireless Technology*. Minneapolis, MN: Lerner Publications, 2009.

Furgang, Kathy. *Netiquette: A Student's Guide to Digital Etiquette*. New York, NY: Rosen Publishing Group, 2010.

Gaines, Ann. *Ace Your Internet Research* (Ace It! Information Literacy). Berkeley Heights, NJ: Enslow Publishers, 2009.

Lester, James, Sr., and James Lester, Jr. *Research Paper Handbook*. 3rd ed. Tucson, AZ: Good Year Books, 2005.

Mercer, David. *The Telephone: The Life Story of a Technology*. Santa Monica, CA: Greenwood Publishers Group, 2006.

Murphy, John. *The Telephone: Wiring America* (Building America: Then and Now). New York, NY: Chelsea House, 2009.

Post Senning, Cindy. *Teen Manners: From Malls to Meals to Messaging and Beyond*. New York, NY: HarperCollins, 2007.

Willard, Nancy. *Cyberbullying and Cyberthreats: Responding to the Challenge of Online Social Aggression, Threats, and Distress*. Champaign, IL: Research Press, 2007.

Willard, Nancy. *Cyber-Safe Kids, Cyber-Savvy Teens*. San Francisco, CA: Jossey-Bass, 2007.

BIBLIOGRAPHY

Breen, Christopher. *The iPhone Pocket Guide*. 4th ed. Berkeley, CA: Peachpit Press, 2010.

Buckleitner, Warren. "Cellphone Etiquette for Kids." *New York Times*, July 21, 2009. Retrieved April 2010 (http://gadgetwise.blogs. nytimes.com/2009/07/21/cellphone-etiquette-for-kids/?scp= 1&sq=cell%20phone%20etiquette%20for%20kids%20warren%20 buckleitner&st=cse).

Clark, Josh. *Best iPhone Apps: The Guide for Discriminating Downloaders*. Sebastopol, CA: O'Reilly Media, 2009.

Faas, Ryan J. *iPhone for Work: Increasing Productivity for Busy Professionals*. New York, NY: Apress, 2009.

Grzywacz, Bogusia. "Number of Cell Phones in the U.S." Hypertextbook. com. Retrieved March 2010 (http://hypertextbook.com/facts/2002/ BogusiaGrzywac.shtml).

Kao, Robert, and Dante Sarigumba. *BlackBerry Storm for Dummies*. Hoboken, NJ: Wiley Publishing, 2010.

McGarvey, Robert J. *Beckett Guide to Phone Apps*. Dallas, TX: Beckett Media, LLC, 2010.

O'Grady, Jason D. *The Google Phone Pocket Guide*. Berkeley, CA: Peachpit Press, 2009.

Rawlinson, Nik. *The Independent Guide to the iPhone 3GS*. London, England: MagBook, 2009.

Reilly, Dan. "Top 10 Cell Phone Myths Explained." Switched.com, March 14, 2008. Retrieved April 2010 (http://www.switched.com/2008/ 03/14/top-10-cell-phone-myths-explained).

Retro Brick. "Motorola DynaTAC 8000x." Retrieved March 2010 (http:// www.retrobrick.com/moto8000.html).

UMTS World. "UMTS/3G History and Future Milestones." Retrieved March 2010 (http://www.umtsworld.com/umts/history.htm).

INDEX

A

Android, 10, 16, 17, 18, 19, 22, 23,
    26, 30
Apple
    iPad, 4, 11, 16, 24
    iPhone, 4, 10, 17, 19, 21, 23, 24,
        26, 30
apps
    for creativity, 30
    for entertainment, 30
    for internet and social networking,
        27–30
    for productivity, 24–27
    purchasing, 28

B

Blackberry, 10, 16, 17, 19, 22, 23, 24,
    26, 30

C

calendars, 20, 22–23
cell phone networks, how they work,
    7–9
cell phones
    etiquette, 31–33
    history of, 4, 6–10
    myths and facts about, 13
Cooper, Martin, 6
copyright, 34
cyberbullying, 35, 36

D

digital librarian, questions to ask a, 37
Digital Reader, Sony, 11
Dropbox, 27

E

EeeKeyboard, ASUS, 11
eReaders, 10–11, 30
Evernote, 26–27

F

Facebook, 29
4G networks, 4, 12
full-duplex communication, 8

G

global positioning systems (GPS), 10,
    29–30
Google
    Gmail, 16
    Mobile, 27
GSM network, 10

H

half-duplex communication, 8

I

instant messaging (IM), 27

About the Author

Colin Wilkinson is a professional video game designer, Web site designer, digital artist, and musician. He enjoys using and learning about new technologies and prides himself on being an early adopter.

Photo Credits

Designer: Nicole Russo; Photo Researcher: Marty Levick